HEALTHY CHOICES

Dinner

Vic Parker

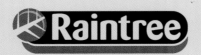

Raintree is an imprint of Capstone Global Library Limited, a company incorporated in England and Wales having its registered office at 7 Pilgrim Street, London EC4V 6LB – Registered company number: 6695582

www.raintreepublishers.co.uk
myorders@raintreepublishers.co.uk

Edited by Rebecca Rissman, Dan Nunn, and
    Diyan Leake
Designed by Philippa Jenkins
Original illustrations © Capstone Global
    Library Ltd 2014
Picture research by Tracy Cummins
Production by Helen McCreath
Originated by Capstone Global Library Ltd
Printed and bound in China

ISBN 978 1 406 27197 3
17 16 15 14 13
10 9 8 7 6 5 4 3 2 1

Parker, Vic
Dinner (Healthy Choices)
A full catalogue record for this book is available from the British Library.

Acknowledgements
We would like to thank the following for permission to reproduce photographs: Capstone Publishers (Karon Dubke) pp. 4, 7, 8, 9, 10, 11, 12, 13, 14, 15, 16, 17, 18, 19, 20, 21, 22, 23, 24, 25, 26, 27; Getty Images pp. 5 (Karl Weatherly), 6 (Fuse).

Cover photograph of roasted salmon with penne and broccoli reproduced with permission of Getty Images (Joseph De Leo) and fish and chips reproduced with permission of Shutterstock (© Joe Gough).

Every effort has been made to contact copyright holders of material reproduced in this book. Any omissions will be rectified in subsequent printings if notice is given to the publisher.

All the internet addresses (URLs) given in this book were valid at the time of going to press. However, due to the dynamic nature of the internet, some addresses may have changed, or sites may have changed or ceased to exist since publication. While the author and publisher regret any inconvenience this may cause readers, no responsibility for any such changes can be accepted by either the author or the publisher.

Contents

Some words are shown in bold, **like this.** You can find out what they mean by looking in the glossary.

Why make healthy choices?

We cannot live for long without food and water. To be healthy, your body needs different kinds of foods, in the right amounts for your age and size. You also need at least six glasses of water every day.

Your brain and body need food and water to be able to think, move, grow, and repair any injuries.

Eating healthy foods helps us to enjoy life.

If you eat healthy food, you will feel and look healthy. If you eat unhealthy food, you will feel and look unhealthy. You may become too thin or **overweight**. You may lack energy and feel tired and grumpy. You may even become ill.

What makes a dinner healthy or unhealthy?

Eating a healthy dinner will fill you up and help you sleep well at night. But some dinners are healthier than others. For instance, beef stew and dumplings can be high in **saturated fat**, which can clog up your heart and blood vessels.

Dinner is the perfect opportunity for your family to spend time together.

To stay healthy, you need to eat the right number of calories for your age, your size, and the amount of exercise you get.

fried beef burgers, creamy mashed potato, buttered peas, onion gravy
800 calories

grilled beef burgers, steamed potatoes and peas
545 calories

Food gives you energy, which is measured in **calories.** Foods can be high or low in calories, depending on what they are and how they are cooked. Eating too many calories at meal and snack times can make you **overweight.** Eating too few can make you too thin.

Meat

Meat is an excellent source of **protein**. Your body needs protein to grow and to repair skin and muscle. However, **red meat,** such as beef steak, can be high in fat, especially if it is fried. Eating it with chips can make your dinner even higher in unhealthy **saturated fat** and **calories.**

Red meat is usually much higher in fat than white meat such as chicken.

fried mushrooms

fried fatty beaf steak

chips

When you can choose, ask for **lean** cuts of red meat rather than fatty cuts.

grilled mushrooms

oven-baked sweet potato wedges with skin on

grilled lean beef steak

Grilling red meat is healthier than frying it, since it does not add fat. You can also grill mushrooms instead of frying them. Choose sweet potato wedges baked with their skin on, rather than chips. These are low in fat and high in **fibre**, which keeps your **digestive system** working properly.

Pizza

Shop-bought pizzas are **processed** foods that contain **artificial additives** such as **preservatives, flavouring,** and **colouring.** Artificial additives can be unhealthy and even harmful. White-flour dough has little **fibre, vitamins,** and **minerals.** Cheese and processed meat are high in **saturated fat** and **sodium.**

processed tomato sauce

white-flour dough

three types of cheese

processed meat

cheese stuffed crust

Half a large stuffed-crust pepperoni pizza contains more **calories** than an eight-year-old needs in a day.

Healthy pizzas are fun to make at home. Prepare a **wholemeal** dough for lots of fibre and long-lasting energy. For toppings full of goodness but low in fat, sodium, and artificial additives, use low-fat cheese, fresh vegetables, and fish.

steamed green vegetables

thin wholemeal crust

low-fat cheese

Pizza can be high in calories, so eat a moderate amount and fill up on healthy salad.

salad

homemade fresh tomato sauce

Pasta

Pasta is full of **carbohydrates,** which give you energy. However, some pasta dinners are much healthier than others. Macaroni cheese is high in **saturated fat, sodium,** and **calories** and low in **fibre, vitamins,** and **minerals.**

Macaroni cheese is tasty as an occasional treat, but it's not healthy as an everyday dinner.

cheesy sauce

white-flour pasta

wholewheat pasta

Wholewheat pasta is healthy and filling.

onions

tomatoes

courgettes

red peppers

yellow peppers

Wholewheat pasta is a good source of healthy fibre. It also releases energy slowly, so it keeps you going for longer. A pasta sauce made of fresh tomatoes and other vegetables, is full of vitamins, minerals, and **antioxidants** that fight disease.

Rice

Rice forms the basis of many dinners. It is a good source of energy and it is low in **saturated fat.** However, it is often eaten in unhealthy ways. For instance, egg fried rice served with sweet and sour pork is high in saturated fat and sugar.

Frying foods adds saturated fat and **calories**.

sugary sweet and sour sauce

deep-fried battered balls of pork

egg fried white rice

Brown rice is even healthier than white rice. This is because it contains seven times as much **fibre.** With a serving of **tofu,** fresh vegetables, and raw nuts, brown rice makes a low-fat meal full of **vitamins, minerals, protein,** and long-lasting energy.

raw peanuts

tofu

broccoli

yellow pepper

red pepper

brown rice

A stir-fry uses very little vegetable oil, so it is a healthy way of cooking.

Fish

Fish is a healthy choice for dinner. It is low in fat but packed with **protein, vitamins,** and **minerals.** Fish has healthy fats that protect the heart. However, certain recipes turn fish into an unhealthy dinner. Frying fish and eating it with chips turns it into a meal high in **saturated fat** and **calories.**

fried fish

chips

Fish and chips is a meal high in calories.

It is good to eat fish at least twice a week. Make sure it is cooked in a healthy way.

boiled brown rice

grilled fish fillet

salad

Choosing an unbattered fillet of fish will give you all of its goodness without adding anything unhealthy. Grilling is a healthy, low-fat way to cook the fish. Boiled rice is much lower in fat than chips. Fresh salad adds vitamins and minerals.

Hot wraps

A tortilla is a round flatbread that can be filled and rolled up to make many kinds of dishes. A burrito is made of a flour tortilla often filled with beef, refried beans, Cheddar cheese, and soured cream. This is a high-**saturated-fat**, high-**calorie** dinner.

white flour tortilla

soured cream

beef

refried beans

Cheddar cheese

A large-sized burrito with fatty fillings is an unhealthy food.

wholewheat tortilla

homemade guacamole

turkey breast

Eat a moderate-sized burrito, so it is not too high in calories. Fill up on healthy salad.

lettuce

tomato

cucumber

kidney beans

sunflower seeds

Swap some ingredients to make your burrito much more healthy. Use a **wholewheat** tortilla, for more **fibre** and longer-lasting energy. Choose a low-fat meat such as turkey instead of beef. Tinned kidney beans, low-fat cheese, and homemade guacamole are low-calorie fillings.

Barbecue

Barbecuing food outside can be a fun way to cook dinner when the weather is hot. However, coating fatty meat in sugary barbecue sauce before it is grilled is not healthy. Salads dressed with mayonnaise and buttered white rolls add even more **saturated fat**, with little **fibre, vitamins,** or **minerals.**

white bread roll with butter

Sauces are often high in fat, with a lot of sugar, salt, or both.

barbecued pork ribs

coleslaw made with mayonnaise

potato salad made with mayonnaise

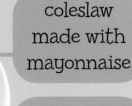

Grilling food outdoors on a barbecue can be a healthy way of eating.

coleslaw made with low-fat yoghurt

wholemeal roll

onion

fish

tomato

red pepper

A much healthier way to barbecue is to grill fish or white meat such as chicken. Avoid coating them in dressings. Threading chunks on skewers with pieces of vegetable makes a colourful meal full of **protein**, vitamins, and minerals. Toss salads in a little low-fat yoghurt and choose **wholemeal** rolls with low-fat spread.

Desserts

A dessert can be a tasty way to round off dinner. However, some desserts, such as shop-bought cakes, can be high in **saturated fat** and **sodium**. Other desserts, such as strawberry pie and ice cream, can be high in saturated fat and sugar.

Many desserts are unhealthy.

high-fat cream

ice cream

high-fat pastry

sugary, high-**calorie** filling

frozen low-fat yoghurt

strawberries

Healthy dessert choices can be delicious.

Fresh fruit with frozen yoghurt is a healthy, tasty dessert. You could also try stirring chopped fresh fruit into a pot of low-fat yoghurt. These desserts are low in saturated fat and filled with **fibre, vitamins,** and **minerals**.

Drinks

Many people like fizzy drinks with their dinner. Some have a milky drink such as a milkshake or cocoa at bedtime. Fizzy drinks are high in sugar. Diet drinks are not much healthier. They are high in **artificial sweetener,** which can be harmful in large amounts. Drinks made with full-fat milk can be high in **saturated fat.**

fizzy drink

cocoa

Full-fat milk and shop-bought juices can be quite high in **calories.**

milkshake

Milky drinks made with semi-skimmed or skimmed milk are much healthier than full-fat milk drinks. They are lower in saturated fat but still high in **calcium**. Your body needs calcium to build strong bones and teeth. Water is a very healthy choice of drink. Every bit of your body needs water to work properly.

water

low-fat milk

Choose a healthy drink to go with your healthy dinner.

Food quiz

Take a look at these roast chicken dinners. Can you work out which picture shows an unhealthy dinner and which shows a healthier dinner, and why?

roast chicken, skin on

shop-bought gravy

roast potatoes

cauliflower cheese

honey-glazed baked carrots

boiled potatoes

roast chicken without skin

homemade gravy

steamed cauliflower

boiled carrots

The answer is on the next page.

Food quiz answers

This is the unhealthy dinner. While there is chicken for **protein**, potatoes for energy, and vegetables for **vitamins** and **minerals,** the cooking methods mean that there is also a lot of **saturated fat** and sugar. Shop-bought gravy often contains a lot of **sodium** as well as fat.

This is the healthy dinner. The roast chicken without the skin is a good source of protein that is lower in fat. Boiling and steaming the vegetables means that no sugar or fat is added. Homemade gravy is much lower in sodium than shop-bought varieties. Did you guess correctly?

Tips for healthy eating

Use this eatwell plate guide to choose the right amounts of different foods for good health. Choose low-fat cooking methods and do not add salt (it is high in **sodium**). Don't forget to drink several glasses of water and to exercise every day.

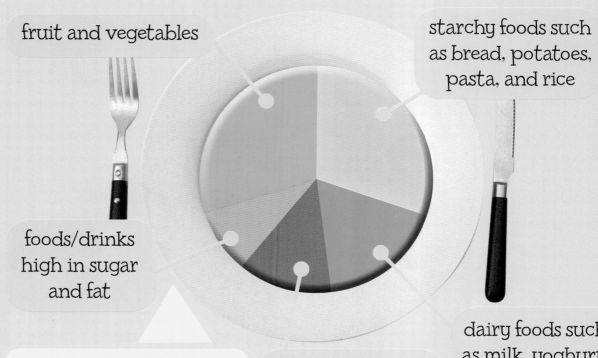

fruit and vegetables

starchy foods such as bread, potatoes, pasta, and rice

foods/drinks high in sugar and fat

dairy foods such as milk, yoghurt, and cheese

protein foods such as meat, fish, eggs, and beans

See if you can get the right balance over the course of a whole day.

Glossary

antioxidant substance that helps your body fight off disease

artificial additive man-made substance that is added to food, such as colouring, flavouring, and preservatives

artificial sweetener man-made substance that can be added to food to give it a sweet taste

calcium a mineral your body needs to build strong bones and teeth. Calcium is found in dairy foods and in some vegetables, nuts, and seeds.

calorie unit we use for measuring energy

carbohydrate substance in starchy foods (such as potatoes, pasta, and rice) and sugary foods that gives you energy

colouring something added to food to make it look attractive

digestive system all the body parts that break down food so the body can use it

fibre part of certain plants that passes through your body without being broken down. This helps other foods to pass through your stomach, too.

flavouring something added to food to make it taste nicer

lean describes meat that has little fat or which has had the fatty bits trimmed off

mineral natural substance, such as iron, that is essential for health

overweight heavier than is healthy for your age and height

preservative something added to food to make it last longer

processed made or prepared in a factory. Processed foods often contain artificial additives.

protein natural substance that your body needs to build skin, muscle, and other tissues. Protein is found in foods such as meat, fish, and beans.

red meat meat such as beef, lamb, and pork, which is red when raw

saturated fat type of fat found in butter, fatty cuts of meat, cheese, and cream. It is bad for your heart.

sodium a natural substance found in salt

tofu a food made from bean curd. It is high in protein and calcium and low in fat and calories.

vitamin natural substance that is essential for good health

wholegrain made with every part of the grain, without removing any of the inner or outer bits

wholemeal made with flour that uses every part of the grain, without removing any of the inner or outer bits

wholewheat made with wheat flour that uses every part of the grain, without removing any of the inner or outer bits